A Tiger Grows Up

by Anastasia Suen ~ illustrated by Michael L. Denman and William J. Huiett

Thanks to our advisers for their expertise, research, and advice:

Janice Owlett, Keeper
Zoological Society of San Diego
San Diego Zoo
San Diego, California

Susan Kesselring, M.A., Literacy Educator
Rosemount–Apple Valley–Eagan (Minnesota) School District

Editorial Director: Carol Jones
Managing Editor: Catherine Neitge
Creative Director: Keith Griffin
Editor: Christianne Jones
Story Consultant: Terry Flaherty
Designer: Nathan Gassman
Production Artist: Angela Kilmer
Page Production: Picture Window Books
The illustrations in this book were created with acrylics.

Picture Window Books
5115 Excelsior Boulevard, Suite 232
Minneapolis, MN 55416
877-845-8392
www.picturewindowbooks.com

Printed in the United States of America.

Library of Congress Cataloging-in-Publication Data
Suen, Anastasia.
A tiger grows up / by Anastasia Suen ; illustrated by Michael Denman and
William J. Huiett.
p. cm. — (Wild animals)
Includes bibliographical references and index.
ISBN 1-4048-0987-2 (hardcover)
1. Tigers—Infancy—Juvenile literature. 2. Tigers—Development—Juvenile literature.
I. Denman, Michael L., ill. II. Huiett, William J., 1943- ill. III. Title.
QL737.C23S855 2006
599.756'139—dc22
2005004282

Welcome to the world of wild animals! Follow a Bengal tiger cub as she grows up in India. From playing in the river to hunting in the tall grass, this young tiger quickly learns to live on her own.

Deep in the forest, a tiny tiger cub is born.
She is much smaller than you were as a baby.
The cub has a new brother and a new sister, too.

The three cubs are helpless. Their mother watches over them in the den.

A mother tiger is called a tigress. A baby tiger is called a cub.

At first, all the cub can do is drink milk and sleep. She can't even open her eyes.

Her mother must hunt for food. The tigress hides her cubs in the shadows when she leaves. Their stripes blend in with the colors of the forest.

Tigers have orange, black, brown, and white stripes. Each tiger has a unique pattern of stripes.

At just one week old, the small cub tries to stand up. Crash! She falls down. She gets up and tries again. She'll learn soon enough.

Young cubs eat and sleep most of the day. They sleep under the trees or in their den.

Since the cubs can't walk, the tigress moves them by holding the scruff of their necks. The skin on the cub's neck is loose, so it doesn't hurt.

On the prowl! The cub is now three months old and can walk.

The tigress brings her cubs meat scraps. The cubs chew the meat with their baby teeth. A tiger cub drinks milk from her mother for about five months.

Tigers are mammals. They drink milk from their mother. As they grow older, they become meat eaters, or carnivores.

At six months old, it's time for the cubs' first hunting lesson. The tigress takes the cubs with her on a hunt. They hide in the grass and watch.

Tigers can see in the dark. They hunt at dusk or early in the morning.

The tigress slowly stalks her prey. She hides in the shadows as it comes near. She quickly pounces on an unsuspecting deer.

In the morning, the tiger cub plays in the river.

Tigers are one of the
few cats that like water.

Splash! The tiger cub catches a fish and eats it.
She is learning to hunt on her own.

A tiger drags its prey to a safe place to eat. One deer can feed a tiger for five or six days.

Look out! The cubs are now strong enough and fast enough to catch animals by themselves.

Tiger cubs stay with their mother until they are about two years old.

Several female tigers may live within a male tiger's territory, but male tigers do not share their territory with other males.

Young tigers often live together after they leave their mother. Soon, they each go off to find their own territories.

At four years old, the young female
tiger is ready to mate and have a family.

In her den, the tigress gives birth to three baby cubs. Just like her mother did for her, the tigress feeds her cubs and keeps them safe. A new family has started in the forest.

Females are ready to mate at three or four years old. Males are ready at four or five years old.

① EARS Tigers have a small white spot on the back of each ear. It looks like another eye.

② EYES Bengal tigers have yellow eyes. White tigers have blue eyes.

③ FEET Tigers can walk without making a sound because of the padding on their feet.

④ FUR A tiger's stripes are on its fur and on its skin.

Map

There are five subspecies of tigers. They live across Asia.
The tigers in this book, the Bengal tigers, live in India.

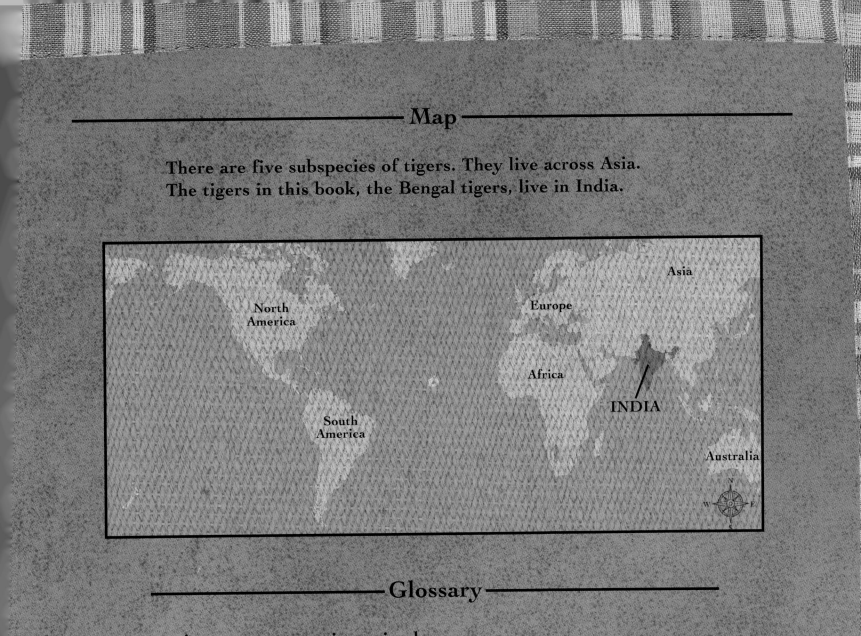

Glossary

carnivore—a meat-eating animal

cub—a baby tiger

mammals—warm-blooded animals that drink milk from
   their mothers

pounce—to leap on something and grip it

prey—an animal that is hunted and eaten by another animal

scruff—loose skin on the back of an animal's neck

stalk—to follow when hunting

territory—the place an animal claims as its own

tigress—a female tiger

To Learn More

At the Library

Barnes, Julia. *101 Facts About Tigers*. Milwaukee: Gareth Stevens Pub., 2004.

Richardson, Adele. *Tigers: Striped Stalkers*. Mankato, Minn.: Bridgestone Books, 2002.

Theodorou, Rod. *Bengal Tigers*. Chicago: Heinemann Library, 2001.

On the Web

FactHound offers a safe, fun way to find Web sites related to this book. All of the sites on FactHound have been researched by our staff. *www.facthound.com*

1. Visit the FactHound home page.

2. Enter a search word related to this book, or type in this special code: 1404809872

3. Click on the FETCH IT button.

Your trusty FactHound will fetch the best sites for you!

Look for all of the books in the Wild Animals series:

A Baboon Grows Up   A Rhinoceros Grows Up

A Hippopotamus Grows Up   A Tiger Grows Up

A Lion Grows Up   An Elephant Grows Up